*This book is dedicated
to all pro-life workers and volunteers—
and especially Caring Families in Danielson, Connecticut*

GERTIE'S NOT ALONE

published by Gold'n'Honey Books
a part of the Questar publishing family

Text and illustrations ©1996 by Normand Chartier
Design by David Uttley

International Standard Book Number: 0-88070-920-0

Printed in the United States of America

For information:
Questar Publishers, Inc. • Post Office Box 1720 • Sisters, Oregon 97759

96 97 98 99 00 01 02 03 — 10 9 8 7 6 5 4 3 2 1

Gertie's Not Alone

NORMAND CHARTIER

Gold 'n' Honey
BOOKS

Inside the henhouse
Gertie Hen sat on her nest.
Inside the nest was an egg,
brown and still and quiet.
Gertie stayed there
to keep the egg warm.

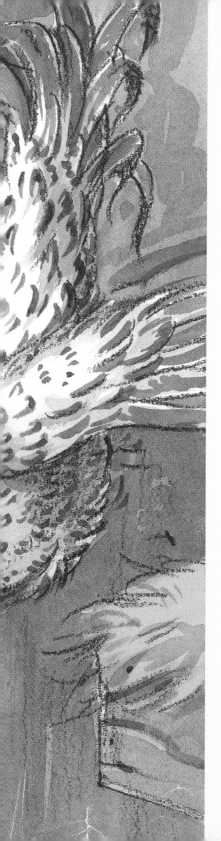

Gertie's rooster
kept bustling in from the barnyard.
He was bringing her favorite food:
crunchy beetlebugs
and juicy grubworms.
"Oh, *thank* you!" Gertie told him.

9

But one morning,
Gertie looked out the henhouse door
with horrified eyes.
Her rooster was being taken away!

"**I** feel so all alone!" Gertie cried.
"I'll have to go out
and find my own food!"
But what about Gertie's egg?
How could she keep it warm?
I'm smart, she thought. *I'm plucky.*
I know I can do it. But how?
Gertie called out
through the henhouse door:
"Help me, someone, please!"

13

The first of her friends
to pop inside the door
was Mottled Molly,
a fine, fancy chicken.
Gertie told Molly her problem.

"Oh," declared Molly,
"that's no problem!
Just do away with it.
After all, it's only an egg."

"I agree," said Surly Sybil,
a bright and bouncy pig.
She pushed in right behind Molly.
"Get rid of it!" she said.

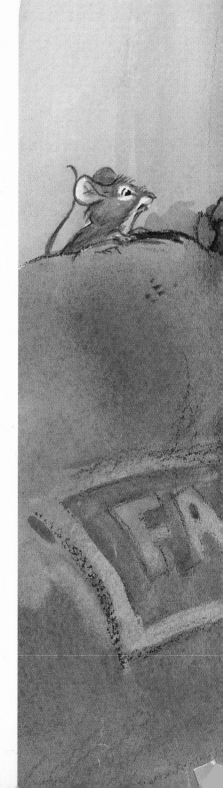

"Yes,"
insisted Grey Goosey Waddle,
who was plump and pleasant.
She plopped through the door
right behind Sybil. "Gertie dear,
you've got to get on with your life.
You must throw that egg away!"

"Oh," said Gertie.
"I guess that's right."

"Oh no, it's *wrong!*"
said Red Rubia, a grandmother hen
who hurried in right behind Goosey.
"Gertie, if you get rid
of your very own egg,
you'll be sad about it forever."

"It will make God sad, too,"
added Lovey Lamb,
who rushed in with Billy G. Goat,
right behind Rubia.

"What's going on here?"
said a little chick named Shelly
with a squeaky little voice.
She slipped in
right under Lovey Lamb,
but no one seemed to notice.

22

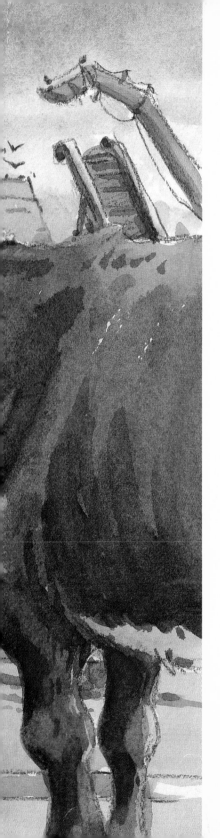

"**D**on't listen to those
old-fashioned folks!" Molly cackled.
And Sybil snorted,
"Remember, it's only an egg!"
And Goosey Waddle honked,
"It's *your* egg, Gertie dear!
You can do whatever you want!"
"NO!" insisted Rubia.
"NO!" insisted Lovey Lamb.
"What egg? Where?"
said Shelly in a squeaky little voice.
But no one seemed to hear her.

25

Dust was rising
and feathers were flying.
Everyone talked and squawked.
"I didn't mean to cause trouble!"
Gertie choked.
She stretched her head
up high where the air was clear.

Suddenly,
a different sort of shout
sounded from somewhere
down in the dust.
The voice was a little squeaky,
but everyone heard it:
"OH!" the voice cried out.
"Just *look!*"

29

When the dust finally settled,
there was Shelly up on the nest
staring at Gertie's egg.
"Look!" she said again.
"It's moving! It's a *miracle!*"
Shelly was right.
The egg was wiggling, just a little bit.
Everybody came closer and stared.
The egg was jiggling, just a little bit.

Then came a noise:
Peckety-peck-peck!
Pickety-packety-peck!
Crackety-crack-CRACK!
Out from the egg
came a little orange beak,
making a little sound:
"Peeky-peep-peep!"
"Why—it *is* a miracle!"
exclaimed Gertie.

33

She wrapped her new baby in her wings.

"He's a fine and fancy chick!" said Molly.

"So bright and bouncy!" added Sybil.

"And so pleasant!" said Goosey Waddle—

"Don't forget to fatten him up, Gertie dear!"

Then Rubia shouted,

"A treasure forever!"

And Lovey Lamb said,

"A gift from God!"

And in a squeaky little voice
Gertie's new baby said,
"Mom, can I go out outside
and play with Shelly?"
"Of course!" answered Gertie,
who never again felt all alone.